Investigate Green Power

Contents

Written by Suzy Senior

Collins

Power

All kinds of things need power, from planes to video games.

We need power for heating and lighting our homes.

Fossil fuels

Today most power comes from fossil fuels.
These include:

gas

coal

crude oil or petroleum

5

How were fossil fuels made?

In prehistoric times, living things died and became crushed by layers of rock. Over time, these turned into oil, gas and coal.

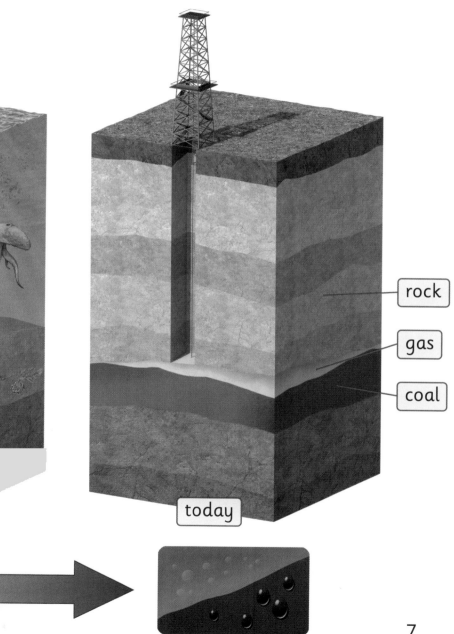

rock

gas

coal

today

7

Running out!

We mine under the land and sea to reach fossil fuels.

drilling rig at sea

But these fuels are finite. This means they will run out one day.

coal mine

A bigger problem

Fossil fuels contain trapped carbon. When we burn these fuels, the carbon inside them escapes as carbon dioxide gas.

This extra carbon dioxide affects the planet.
Extreme heat and storms now happen often.

Crops die in fields due to extreme heat and no rain.

What can we do?

We need to create cleaner, greener power.

These kinds of power can be renewed,
so they won't run out.

Solar power

Solar panels create electric power from sunshine.
They can be in fields or on houses.

Even lamp-posts can have solar panels.

Water power

Water can drive a turbine. The turbine rotates and creates electric power.

The river drives turbines inside this concrete dam.

turbine

Wind power

Wind can drive turbines to create electric power.

Wind turbines stand in fields, on houses, or even at sea.

19

Underground heat

Far underground, there are hot rocks!

Water piped over them turns into steam.
This steam drives a turbine, making electric power.

Flower power!

The fuel in most cars comes from crude oil.
But we can make cleaner fuels, like biogas
and biodiesel.

Eco fuels are made from sunflower, peanut and soya bean oils!

Nuclear power: green or not?

When nuclear fuels react, they make heat. Just a little can create lots of power, without extra carbon dioxide.

However, they are finite, and the waste can harm us. Some waste must be kept safe for thousands of years!

Making electric power across the planet

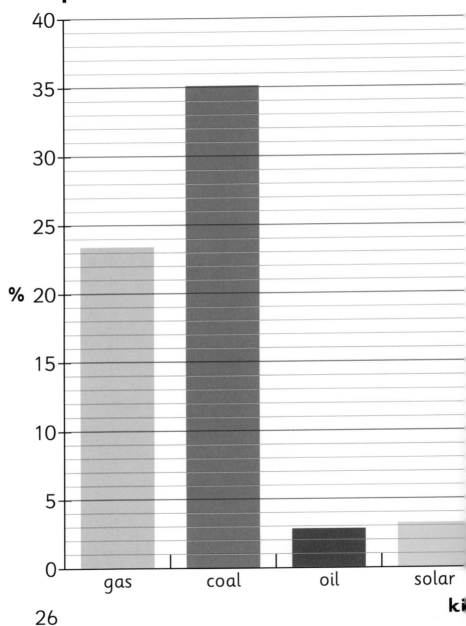

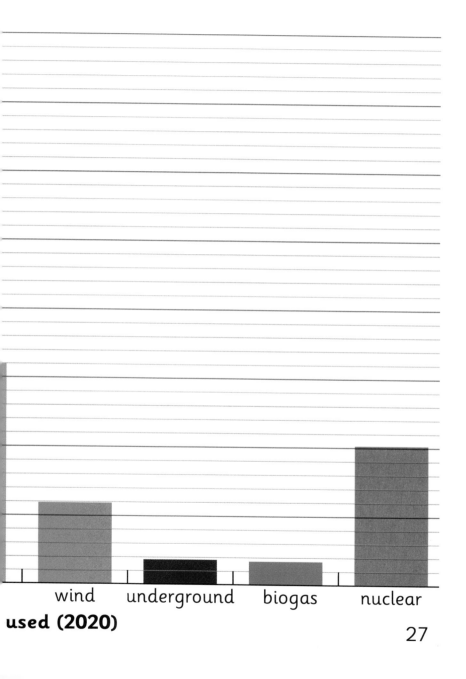

wind   underground   biogas   nuclear

used (2020)

Kielder Water

turbir

There are turbines at Kielder Water in the UK.

Each day, the power the turbines create could light up an entire town.

Green power

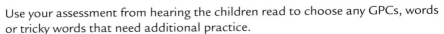

Review: After reading

Use your assessment from hearing the children read to choose any GPCs, words or tricky words that need additional practice.

Read 1: Decoding

- Encourage the children to practise reading words that contain one or more of the new sounds, breaking them into syllable "chunks" if necessary.

  pet/rol/e/um   **vid/e/o**   **di/ox/ide**   **fin/ite**   **cre/ate**   **re/newed**

  o Ask them to take turns to find more words with /ee/, /igh/ or /oa/ sounds and identify the spellings.

- Ask the children to choose a page to read aloud. Encourage fluency by asking them to sound out words in their heads as they read.

Read 2: Prosody

- Point out how we can use emphasis to connect words with what's been written earlier. Model reading the title on page 10, emphasising **bigger**. Say: This connects with the smaller problems we've already read about.

- Discuss how **these** on page 10 refers back to **fossil fuels** in the previous sentence.

- Challenge the children to read pages 10 and 11, using emphasis to connect words and ideas.

Read 3: Comprehension

- Ask the children what they already know about the problems around power. Ask: Do you do anything to save power?

- Look at pages 30 and 31, and talk about the pictures. Can the children identify the kind of power that each picture relates to?

- Bonus content: Ask the children to look at pages 26 and 27, and decide what the author of the book would think about the kinds of power that are most often used. Would she be happy or unhappy? Why?